THE TROPHIES OF GRACE

LIONEL ETWARU

WestBow Press
A DIVISION OF THOMAS NELSON
& ZONDERVAN

Copyright © 2014 Lionel Etwaru.

All rights reserved. No part of this book may be used or reproduced by any means, graphic, electronic, or mechanical, including photocopying, recording, taping or by any information storage retrieval system without the written permission of the publisher except in the case of brief quotations embodied in critical articles and reviews.

WestBow Press books may be ordered through booksellers or by contacting:

WestBow Press
A Division of Thomas Nelson & Zondervan
1663 Liberty Drive
Bloomington, IN 47403
www.westbowpress.com
1 (866) 928-1240

Because of the dynamic nature of the Internet, any web addresses or links contained in this book may have changed since publication and may no longer be valid. The views expressed in this work are solely those of the author and do not necessarily reflect the views of the publisher, and the publisher hereby disclaims any responsibility for them.

Any people depicted in stock imagery provided by Thinkstock are models, and such images are being used for illustrative purposes only. Certain stock imagery © Thinkstock.

ISBN: 978-1-4908-3928-8 (sc)
ISBN: 978-1-4908-3929-5 (e)

Library of Congress Control Number: 2014910272

Printed in the United States of America.

WestBow Press rev. date: 06/20/2014

CONTENTS

PREFACE   Rev. Kenneth Ragoonath, President of Open Bible Institute of Theology in Trinidad; Member of HCF International Board; Chairman of the Operation Mobilization Board. vii

ACKNOWLEDGEMENTS ix

FOREWORD By Bishop Marcus Roberts, Senior Pastor of Calvary Cathedral of Praise in Brooklyn, New York City xi

Chapter One   MY PERSONAL TESTIMONY 1

Chapter Two   THE APOSTLE HARRY DAS 9

Chapter Three THE CORENTYNE CONNECTION 14

Chapter Four   THE TEAM FACTOR, CONNECTING WITH THE LATE APOSTLE PHILIP MOHABIR 40

Chapter Five   THE BIBLE TRAINING CENTER 46

Chapter Six   THE INTERNATIONAL CONNECTIONS .. 61

Chapter Seven	THE UNKNOWNS (SOME UNSUNG HEROES)	96
Chapter Eight	THE LESSONS	105
Chapter Nine	THE NON-NEGOTIABLES	109
THE CONCLUSION		113

PREFACE

It was my pleasure to meet Lionel Etwaru on December 11, 1974, through the reference of another friend. I met him on my first trip to Guyana, the Beautiful Land of Many Waters. He was at the Airport to receive me. That was a great relief, being in a strange land.

I was there on Hospital Christian Fellowship business. He was willing to be my host, chauffeur and guide. For many days, we drove from one end of the Coast of the country to the other, visiting the main Hospitals, and making contact with Administrators and the Christians in the institutions. I was very impressed by what I saw him and a team of dedicated men and women doing for the Kingdom of God. He was, then, the Principal of the Bible Training Center and Chairman of the Ful Gospel Fellowship of Churches. They were busy preaching the Gospel in the villages across the country, leading men and women to Christ, and planting churches.

Through his instrumentality, I came in contact with some very important and resourceful people. Some became an integral part of the founding of HCF in Guyana. They became the backbone for the existence and growth of HCF in Guyana. I still have strong relational and working connections with most of these people. One outstanding couple has been the late Victor Dayalsingh and his wife, Esther. Many are now residing in other countries. We are still in contact.

His outstanding Leadership capabilities have not only enabled him to make an indelible impact in Guyana, but in other nations around the world. He has a special way of preaching the Word of God with great zeal and animated enthusiasm. Many around the world have been blessed by his ministry.

He has made a sterling contribution since 1963 in the founding and establishment of the Full Gospel Fellowship, and its connections in many other countries. He surely deserves to be recognized and honored as they celebrate the Golden Anniversary of the Full Gospel Fellowship.

I am sure that this book will make a dynamic impact to remind us all of the Goodness and Greatness of God, and be a means of Inspiration to the Next Generation. It will establish that God who has begun a Good work over these decades can continue to perform and perfect it until the Day of His Appearing.

By Kenneth Ragoonath, from Trinidad. President of Open Bible Institute of Theology; Member of HCF International Board.

ACKNOWLEDGEMENTS

To my dear wife and my two daughters who have always pushed me to write. To one special young man, Mark King, in the church I pastor, who would constantly egg me on to stop talking and do it.

I also do this to honor the two men who made a great impact in my life—Apostle Harry Das under whose ministry, I became a Christian, and who was extremely instrumental in my early Discipleship nurture. He has always been an immense source of inspiration and challenge until this day.

I give duely earned honor to the late Apostle Philip Mohabir. He had been more a spiritual father and mentor. He was surely responsible for most of what I have become in God and in my ministry. He always made you feel that he has confidence in you and you can excel.

I must say thanks to a young lady from the church in Linden. She made it her business to meet me after I spoke in a Leaders Conference at the Cultural Center in Georgetown, and boldly and emphatically said to me, " You owe us to put those things in a book. I have been in this Fellowship for the past ten years and have not heard those names and some of the things you mentioned." Hence this book!

Of course, all the Glory and Honor belong to the Lord Jesus Christ who loved me so much that He chose me at a very crucial time in my life and allowed me to be a Trophy of His Grace, and be integrally involved in the Evangelization of Guyana and many other nations.

TO HIM BE ALL THE GLORY AND HONOR FOREVER AND FOREVER!

FOREWORD

I feel honored to have the privilege of writing the foreword for this particular book written by Apostle Lionel Etwaru.

First of all, because of my Friendship and Fellowship with him and his family dating back many years. I have found him to be a man of humility, Integrity, and deep spirituality- a man dearly loved by his peers and people in general from many nations. I have had the privilege of holding crusades with him in Guyana, as well as staying in their home. He has a wonderful family.

Secondly, a book of this nature is overdue, and will be greatly appreciated. The Full Gospel Fellowship of Churches and Ministers have made a great impact on many nations. Their Bible Training Center has produced great preachers and teachers who have impacted many nations, and planted numerous churches around the world.

The History of the Full Gospel Fellowship is very rich in Content. How it started? Who were the Founders and the Visionaries? – the tremendous growth from small Beginnings.

TO GOD BE THE GLORY—GREAT THINGS HE HAS DONE!

By Bishop Marcus Roberts, Calvary Cathedral of Praise.

CHAPTER ONE
MY PERSONAL TESTIMONY

I can never forget the words that have stuck with me ever since, "What manner of man is this that even the winds and waves obey him." Evangelist Harry Das in his animated, vivacious and dynamic fashion proclaimed, as he was preaching on the story of Jesus stilling the storm recorded in the Gospel of Mark 4:41. This was the sixth night of my being at these religious meetings. I have spent much time during these nights as a heckler with two of my friends. We must have been a great nuisance, as we would scream out, "He could not save Himself, how could He save us," when the preacher would say Jesus came to be our Savior. This we did as we stood in the dark of the precincts of the meeting place.

I ended up in these meetings because my late sister, Elsie, began attending them at the invitation of a friend. My parents were not happy that a young woman has been out so late over these nights. This was in the early sixties, when it was felt in the villages that no decent single young woman should be so late in the streets. So, the only compromise for my sister was that I accompany her. The reason I consented was that I could blackmail her for money and other favors. These were my trump cards. I did not realize that God was fixing a fix to fix me up for life. I met my two friends at the meeting. Most of the time, we were having our own meeting.

On that sixth night, in September 1963, which would become momentous and unforgettable, one of my friends encouraged us to go up closer when people were asked to come to the front of the stage for prayer. We went up together. We were still giggling, whispering and elbowing each other. We were not serious. Then the preacher, the Rev. Harry Das came around by us and asked if we will be reverent for a few moments and repeat a prayer after him. For some reason I said a few words. The meeting concluded. I went home. I tried to complete my home work, as I was still in High School. I was attending the very reputable Corentyne High School. Something strange began to happen, I felt like I was just seeing the whole meeting on a television screen. Momentarily, I felt scared, and then at peace, not understanding what was happening. I did not want to wake up my parents lest they will be angry and declare that some evil spirits have followed us home. That will mean we cannot go back to the meetings. I went into bed and tried to sleep. I could not sleep. So, I decided to pray. I went on my knees, and then realized I did not know what to pray. It came back to my mind, some of the things the preacher said that you can say if you want to pray. I can remember, as if it were yesterday, the few words I said, "Lord, if you can do all that those people talk about, please do it for me." I felt His transforming power working in me. I began to feel different.

The next day at school, I could not do the kind of things I used to do and say with my friends. They could not understand what had happened to me. I could not explain it either. Of course, to be in a class with forty one other teenagers who knew you to be one way and suddenly there seemed to be an inexplicable difference was another issue. It did not make sense. Some of them knew that I was attending these meetings. So they made their own conclusions.

Then, the taunting and persecution began. They were telling all the teachers that, "Etwaru has joined the Brother Das church and the clap hand church." It was very tough. Sometimes, I felt embarrassed, but now I understand that it had to be the Lord who helped me through those times.

At home, the pressure was on also. My parents, especially, my dad was very upset that I became a christian. They felt that both my sister and I were a disgrace to the family to change our religion. My dad was so angry that one day he said to me, "I should have planted one more coconut tree, than having you as a son." This, in our Indo-Guyanese culture was a great insult. Eventually, he changed his mind. My close friends gave me one week to recant, then a month, then a semester, even one year. They had to give up. I always remember meeting one of my teachers from High school some years later. He asked me, "Etwaru, are you still keeping up the church thing?" I responded respectfully, "The church thing is keeping me up, sir."

One outstanding thing happened a few weeks after my conversion. I was able to lead my best friend and classmate Doodnauth Ramdass, to the Lord. He still serves the Lord today in Ajax, Canada.

I have always been happy for the opportunity to be a child of God and to be alongside the founding fathers of Full Gospel Fellowship in Guyana. The Lord allowed me to come through the ranks, from Sunday School teacher to leading meetings. Then later, I functioned in a pastoral role, helping in some of the newly founded churches. I was the local youth leader and one of the first National Youth Leaders of the Guyana Youth Aflame when it began in August1966. This was the youth arm of the Full Gospel Fellowship. I was an Elementary School Teacher, at the Cropper Government School, in my village, Albion Front, for three years, before resigning and entering the ministry fulltime in August 1969. I was immediately appointed Assistant Principal alongside the late Apostle Philip Mohabir, in the Full Time Training Program. I served in that capacity, then as Principal and Director before migrating to the USA in 1989. I was also Chairman and Treasurer of the Fellowship for a number of years.

The Call For Full-Time Ministry

From the time, I became a Christian I got involved in church activities. I, somehow desired to be involved. I helped my Sister, Elsie, in a Sunday School, she was teaching with about seventy kids. The church had thirty Sunday Schools in the neighboring villages. This was a great way of reaching the kids and their parents. These schools were held in the lower level of homes, which we called, "bottom houses."

When my sister left, I took over the Sunday School, although, I had no formal training as such. The zeal of the Lord and His house propelled me. In 1965, I received the first prophetic word of God's call on my life for ministry.

The most dramatic experience in my life happened in our Youth Camp of 1969 in Kuru Kuru along the Linden Highway. In the penultimate night of the camp, a word of knowledge came forth that

God was calling a young man. I felt nothing. Of course, I was one of the Camp leaders, and thought it could not be me. Two young men went up and the preacher, Dennis Hilliman said he was happy for them, but they were not the young man. By then, I began to feel a tug of the Spirit of God in my heart. I started weeping, but will not go forward. Two other prophecies came forth. They were strong. The Lord was saying the person had three months to live. I began weeping loudly, but will not go forward. Then Apostle Das strongly addressed me that if God was dealing with me why I would not obey. I responded, " I want to come but I cannot walk." The Apostle said, " Bring him." I remembered that brothers Mohammed Yasim and Winston Campbell helped me to the altar, which was about ten feet away. They did not realize that I could not stand. They let go of me and I dropped on the ground…..no wooden floor or plush carpet. No catchers, like we have today. It was all beach sand, possibly with some stumps. God began to deal with me to yield that night. I fought and struggled and wanted to just say, "I surrender," but my will was not. Something horrible happened at that moment. I felt God took away my speech. I wanted to speak but no words were coming out. I, then began to make loud howling sounds. The entire group of about four hundred youths were praying and weeping, and broken before God.

My Will finally surrendered. I felt my speech returned, and I began calling on God. I gave up totally to Him and His Will. No words can describe the peace and confidence I experienced. I also felt that the thunderous voice I have was bestowed on me at that moment.

By His grace, there has not been even an iota of a thought of going back. I have never had a doubt of God's Cali. I supposed that all who were there have never had doubts. Folks constantly relate how awesome that night was.

His all-sufficient Grace and loving kindness have kept me over these decades. I am fully persuaded that the Lord who has kept me to this time, will preserve me to the end.

My Partner For Life

My wife and I – 1977

Marriage seemed to have been in the back burner for many years. I was so involved in the work of God during those pioneering days, and my Pastor, Apostle Harry Das always put marriage at the bottom of the list of priorities. He would teach on the call of God, and the Imminent Return of the Lord, then he would list marriage last. So, by the time you hear all of that and consecrate your life for those things, time was up. The class ended. But, it did well for us over those years and until now. It made us to have a very balanced perspective of life.

Most of my contemporaries finally did get married. I even officiated at some of their weddings and of those members I raised up in the churches. Yet, I was unmarried. It happened suddenly. I have known Margaret ever since I came in the church. I always admired her for her commitment, dedication to God, and her involvement in the work of God. Of course, she has always been very pretty.

Her involvement in the church was expressed in her being the Pastor of the Rose Hall church for a number of years. During those years, she was also a professional banker with Barclays Bank. It was not until March 1975, that I began to feel something different for her. After some time of prayer, I popped the question. She responded positively. I went the traditional way. I wrote a letter to her mom, asking Margaret's hand in marriage. We got engaged on her birthday, July 7, 1975.

Margaret, on the other hand, testified that God had shown her very clearly over a period of two years that I was to be her husband. So, she put some fleeces before the Lord. One of them was that if it was God's will then I must write a letter to her mom asking her hand in marriage. I did that, without knowing. We, finally got married on August 1, 1977, and are still very happily married.

The Vision

David Tomlinson, a friend from England once said, it is important that people BUY the Vision and OWN it, not just RENT or LEASE it. I was one of the people who unreservedly bought the Vision. It was a TOTAL INVESTMENT. I became a part of it, and it became an integral and consuming part of me.

The early group of workers also bought the Vision to live by faith, Reach the Villages and Towns with the Gospel and Plant AUTONOMOUS AND INDIGENOUS churches. The first month, I resigned my job as a School Teacher, the newly pioneered church in Bath Settlement gave me $28.00 (Guyana). As an Elementary School Teacher, I used to earn $142.50 (Guyana). That was a lot of money in those days. The rent for the house we were using for living and the church was $300.00 (Guyana). I immediately and reverently told the Lord, " You will have to do better, if not I will consider going back to my job." That was daring and facetious but I was very desperate. We thanked God for the precious saints who brought us cooked and delicious meals almost every day.

I have learnt over the years, that the same God who can provide $20.00, can provide $2000.00, $200,000.00, and now I am believing God for more than $2,000,000.00 to pay off for our present church property, in Richmond Hill, Queens, New York.

HE is indeed our JEHOVAH JIREH, "The Provider." I have lived long enough to be able to declare, **"HE NEVER FAILS!"**

CHAPTER TWO
THE APOSTLE HARRY DAS

The Man Used By God

Apostle Harry Das, Mama Das and their son John

In those days, everyone knew him as" Brother Das". That name, almost became a household name in that part of Guyana, the

Corentyne coast and eventually the whole of the County of Berbice, known as the "Ancient County"

Today, we honor and recognize him as Apostle Harry Das. He has surely and deservedly earned such a title.

I would always remember him relating a dream he had of being in Heaven, and was ushered in a room filled with Trophies. He said he had difficulties walking among them, as there were so many, representing his tremendous achievements on earth.

He was born and raised in a staunch Hindu home. If fact, he belonged to what was deemed the highest cast in that religion. The group from which the priests are appointed. But, God had other plans. He came in contact with a God- fearing Christian woman, who was fondly called, Mother Harper. It was in her home that he received Jesus Christ as his personal Savior. He and a handful of others were surely among the first to have experienced the Pentecostal Outpouring of the Holy Spirit in Guyana.

Through much persecution, he grew in God. He himself became a pastor with the Assemblies of God group of churches, in Guyana, in one of the areas of the Capital City, Georgetown. There were a number of outstanding men and women of God in those times whom he was instrumental in raising up for the ministry. If I am not mistaken, his wife sister Cora Allen was among them. He was instrumental in leading most if not all of his siblings to the Lord, and eventually his parents before the Lord called them home.

Sometime in the late 1950's, the world renowned Evangelist/Prophet Morris Cerullo, came to Guyana. Apostle Harry Das was the Co-ordinator of the meetings, and sister Cora Allen was leading the choir.

After these meetings, he heard and felt the clarion call of God to evangelize his country. His burden was to travel to the villages and towns and preach the Gospel to the lost. He began in the bauxite mining town of Mackenzie, now called Linden. His meetings were held in the section called Wismar. There are a number of people alive today who testify about the outstanding miracles that were wrought and the numerous souls that got converted into the Kingdom of God. He did not start a church there but referred the converts to some of the existing churches.

In my book, he has to be noted as the first National Evangelist/Pioneer, Guyana has known. He must also be the most outstanding Evangelist this country has ever produced. The study of the New Testament model Evangelist, Phillip in Acts chapter 8, will surely describe Evangelist Harry Das in those days.

Any Christian who has known him and was able to get close enough to him will definitely agree with me that he has been a "Man of Prayer." I would feel that all his success in breaking new territories for the Kingdom of God in Guyana and many other Nations has to be contributed to Persistent Prayer. Guys who knew him in those early days would try to hide from him if they saw him walking in the same street with them. They were afraid that he would call them to pray in the street. He prayed while driving. He would be praying in the Spirit most of the night. Before he counseled someone he would pray first, and sometimes by the end, the counselee would feel that God had already given them the answer.

He was not only a Man of Prayer, Fasting was also a hallmark of his ministry.

While many would bask after a successful meeting, especially crusade, by joking and rehearsing the funny things, and maybe some good things, he would call you to pray that God would preserve the souls and ward off demonic onslaughts from bombarding them with doubts and discouragement. These meetings would go on all night sometimes.

He had a consuming burden for the lost souls of men and women. He interceded constantly. He would weep for hours. He would groan for hours upon hours. Daniel Mootoo was a hard working man but he loved drinking. While the crusade was going on in his yard in Albion Front, (that is where I got saved), he would come home drunk. Apostle Harry Das after the meeting, would kneel by the hammock, and pray for Mootoo's salvation as he slept.

I remembered him coming to my home late one night, after a crusade meeting to visit my Hindu father. He and two other brothers who knew my father. The brothers talked with my dad about some old time stories. The Apostle prayed, and they left. The next night my dad went to the crusade and God gloriously saved him and delivered him from an alcoholic habit. Trophies of grace, hallelujah!

Apostle Das had a unique vision when he came to the Corentyne. Together, with crusades in the nights, he targeted the schools in the days. He reached for the next generation. My colleagues and I were that generation. We took on the baton when he left. We continued to invade the schools with the Gospel, and the villages with crusades and planting churches.

His vision was bigger than Guyana. He went to the USA and Canada and helped to plant churches and ministered in many others. Then he moved on to Africa where he spent many years. He returned in the 1980's to pastor a church in Newport News, Virginia. He set up a new base and served the foreign fields while he led the church in Virginia. Today, I feel that he oversees the local church, and his only son, Evangelist/Pastor John Das does more of the day to day ministry with the Elders and other leaders. The Apostle Das also gives Apostolic covering to the foreign fields via the many outstanding men and women he has raised up over the past decades. An Apostle indeed! Numerous Trophies of Grace to celebrate!

Apostle Harry Das (front far right) with a team of men from the church

CHAPTER THREE
THE CORENTYNE CONNECTION

The Sewdin's Home in Rose Hall Town, where the church began - 1961

In 1961, Apostle Das headed for the Ancient County, called Berbice, Guyana. This is on the eastern section of the country bordering Surinam. He, and a small team in a Morris Station Wagon headed for New Amsterdam, the second largest city.

This was a British made vehicle. On both front doors and the back were praying hands with the words "PRAY OR PERISH" written boldly. I must mention that this was a giant step of faith. They hardly knew where they would stay and how long. Their first place of lodging was a funeral home. He and his team were given rooms on the second floor of a funeral home. During the day, he would drive around and spy out the land. He eventually went to a more easterly village called Gibraltar, where he slept in his Station Wagon by the roadside for a few nights. The Campbell's family got in touch with him and gave him a place in their home where they slept on wooden benches for a few nights. Of course, during this time they were busy sharing the gospel and leading souls to Christ. Brother Campbell testified that he got saved and filled with the Holy Ghost in one shot. What a glorious story. Brother Campbell and some of the new believers made them mattresses stuffed with a popular grass called "iron grass." Apostle Harry Das did not stop there. He related that God showed him a chubby woman. He must find her. She would help him further. That woman was the late sister Kate Sewdin. She became fondly known as Auntie Kate. She opened her home for at least nine months to this complete stranger but surely outstanding Servant of God. A number of godly men and women found rest in this home in Rose Hall Town, Corentyne. In fact the church in the Corentyne was born in this home.

The team eventually rented the second flat of a lemonade factory. Brother Eddie Ramsammy, his wife Shirley, one of my sisters, and family gave themselves to live and serve the team for a few years.

As the church began to grow in Rose Hall Town, Apostle Das rented an old cinema, called " the Cosmopolitan" in late 1962. Every Sunday, believers from the surrounding villages gathered here. During the week, services…...Bible Study, Prayer Meetings and other activities were held in what were called "Out Stations." This was a great means of Evangelism and the development of ministries. Then eventually, as the out-stations grew, they were set up as local churches.

From here as a base, the Apostle went from village to village holding crusades. He went to Gibraltar. There is a church still there today with a beautiful building, pastored by Phillip Campbell. Fyrish was the next stop. Many got saved, healed and delivered from demonic powers. A church was planted and still goes on. He moved to my village, Albion Front. That was where I got saved with many others. May I note these were not re-cycled saints. They were lost in many religious beliefs and many possessed and affected by demons. A number of families came to the Lord. The late Daniel Mootoo, and his entire family surrendered to the lordship of Christ. It was in his yard the crusade was held where I got saved. He was also second in command in the Kali Temple in that village, before he became a christian. The Ponen's family and the Kisten's and many others; too many to mention came into the Kingdom of God.

Crusades were held in Rose Hall; Port Mourant; Tain Settlement; No. 48 and 56 villages; Corriverton; Bush Lot and Chesney. Churches were founded in all of these areas. Churches that are still alive and vibrant today. At one time we were in lower flats of houses, called, "bottom houses." Today, there are beautiful and architecturally designed church buildings to mark the works of God, and the faithfulness of dedicated men and women.

The Trophies of Grace

Water Baptism at 63 Beach

People called us many names: " the clap hand church," "brother Das church," "the church where they cry, and make a lot of noise and pray loudly as if God is deaf."

Apostle Harry Das left for seventeen days for the USA in 1971. Those days never ended it seemed. He got married to his long time fiancee, sister Cora Allen while in the USA. He told us that he waited thirteen years for this to happen. PRAISE GOD!

Apostle Harry and Cora Das – on their Wedding Day
(To the left of Apostle Harry Das is Pastor Harry Binda)

Farewell Service for Apostle Harry Das – 1971

The work he began just continued. The team of men and women he raised up continued to blaze the trail. Brothers Desmond Singh, Victor Raghunath, Vishnu Shiwpal, Winston Campbell, the Bickram's family, the Sewdin's, the Bhajan's and a list of many others, too many to mention…...all Trophies of Grace….pursued the vision.

Today, there are at least Fourteen vibrant and growing churches that are part of the Full Gospel Fellowship, plus a number of others that were founded by him and his leaders that he raised up. Some churches are not particularly connected to the Fellowship.

The Canaan Full Gospel Church

This name was given because the whole compound was available for us to purchase in 1967. We were not able to do it. This ten acre plot was divided into house lots. When my wife and I returned to the Corentyne in January 1979 to lead the district, the church in Rose Hall was meeting in the second floor of a building owned by the Bhajan's family. I took on the pastoral responsibility, and served the church and the district until my family and I migrated to the USA in 1989. We purchased two lots in the compound in Port Mourant and erected the building that is there now.

Canaan Full Gospel Church

My Wife Leading Praise and Worship

Dedication of the Canaan Church Building

Myself, Family and Congregation

We called it, "**CANAAN**" because of the length of time it took us to secure it. This was a fulfillment of a prophetic word that was given by Apostle Harry Das. The word was that we will have a Convention and Conference Center, an Orphanage and a Nursing Home. I was able to build the Center, and secure a property in the compound for an Orphanage in the 1980's. I changed it from Orphanage to Children's Home. Orphanage carries a psychological stigma to it. I felt that the children needed a normal and regular home environment.

The Children's Home

Sis. Mona and the First Group of Children

This was the main church founded by Apostle Harry Das. Today, it is still growing and moving on under the pastoral care of Vernon D'oliviera.

Ministering in Crusade at the Albion Complex
with Evangelist Jerry and Theresa Wolcson

The Corentyne Ministry Team

There was a large team of men and women who labored with Apostle Harry Das, and continued the work after he left. Of course, Apostle Mohabir was very integrally involved, and took this region under his leadership also.

His late sister Lily Prasad and her late husband were an integral part of that team. The late brother Sonny Bickram and his entire family labored conscientiously and served without reservation in many areas for the growth of the work. He was one of the first elders with brother Peter Singh in the church. He accommodated the Port Mourant church in a building by his house free of charge for many years. The Ramotar Singh's family also served sacrificially.

Desmond Singh became the first leader of the team of workers in the Corentyne. He served until he resigned and migrated to Canada.

Brother David Dwarka labored from 1975 to 1979, succeeding Desmond Singh, until he migrated to Canada. He continued with his wife, sister Kema, to pastor there, until they retired a few years ago.

Brother Victor Raghunath has also been there from the beginning. He served as Sunday School teacher, leader of groups that we used to call outstations. He was also involved in the National Youth movement, taught in the Bible School and functioned as Registrar, until he migrated to the USA, with his wife, Sandra to further their studies in Theology. Today they pastor a church, which they have pioneered in Queens, New York.

Ramseywack Somai, was also saved from Hinduism in those early days. He endured much persecution at the hands of family and friends. He served in many small areas in the church until he became a Pastor, Bible School teacher, District leader and Assistant Superintendent of the Fellowship, until he and his family migrated to the USA.

In the 1980's to date, there has been a long list of men and women who have been raised up and some imported to continue to build in the Corentyne. I would like to list a few: the late Cecil and Ivy Mohabir; Wally Sasenarine; Vernon and Veera D'oliveira; Mohammed Mursalin; Rishi and Padminie Timram; Roy and Shirley Roberts; Roop and Lorie Mangroo; Rommel and Ramona Etwaroo, Dwarka and his wife, and many others whose names are already recorded in heaven. This changing of guards, as it were, has just been extremely remarkable for the continuation for what God had begun.

I must mention one of my faithful sons, Francis Sahadupal and his wife Francine. He was with me at Canaan from the very beginning. He willingly and sacrificially served until I migrated to the USA. Then, in the early 1990's he pioneered his own church that he is now leading in Haswell, Corentyne. The name of the church is "God of the Change International church."

Myself with Pastors Desmond and Victor

Myself with Pastors Somai and Victor

The Trophies of Grace

Myself, the late Pastor Seodat, Sis. Anita, the late Elder Bickram and Pastor Ramkissoon

Apostle Harry Das Preaching

Trophies of the Gift of Giving (a Special Area)

I feel that I need to recognize a number of believers who contributed plots of Land free of charge so that we could have built some of the buildings we have. I am proud of them, (for the want of a better expression.) To God be the Glory for these Trophies of the Grace of Giving.

Brother Roopnarine and family from Bloomfield, who did not only give land to the church in Letter Kenny, but built the original church building which was quickly out grown.

First Church in Letter Kenny

Brother Peter Ramsuchit.and family who gave the plot where the church building now stands in Letter Kenny.

Brother Somwaru, his wife sister Kamla and family who gave their house lot to the church in Bush Lot, so we can have the building that is there as a testimony for the King of kings.

Thanks to Brother Kennard and his family in Farm Village, for the many years they allowed us to hold meetings, free of charge, by their home.

Mr. And Mrs. Gopaul and family from Cotton Tree who contributed a house lot in No. 56 village, so that we can have that church building there today.

The Singh's family in No. 48 village for allowing us to use the first floor of their home for many years without charge. Today, Apostle Rishi Timram has built a beautiful building and is pastoring the church with his wife Padmini.

First Meeting Place in Number 48 Village

The Khan's family in Corriverton also availed the first level of their home for the church for a number of years, free of charge.

Commendation must be given to the late Harold Ramsammy and family, in Cromarty, for allowing us, free of charge, to hold church meetings in a building they provided for many years.

Recognition must be given to my friend Pastor Michael Dillman, his wife Jan and the church in Modesto, California. They gave the Seven Thousand US Dollars that was needed to purchase the Belvedere Property in 1984.

Pastor Michael Dillman and I

Belvedere Full Gospel Church

Number 56 Church

Number 48 Church

Church at Corriverton

West Coast Berbice

From the Corentyne, I must have been the first missionary that was sent out to pioneer churches in West Coast Berbice. This mission began in Bath Settlement, and was the direct inspiration from our first National Youth Camp that was held in Stanleytown, West Bank Demerara in August 1966. There were about thirty-five campers, drawn mostly from Corentyne and West Demerara.

This was a special camp. Of course, it was the first. That is when the name was coined, "Guyana Youth Aflame." That was also, when the late Apostle \Mohabir passed on the vision of reaching the lost to this group of youths. So, Neville Solomon and I were commissioned to West Coast Berbice. He left after a few weeks. I was left alone to pursue the task. I was able to lead my cousin, Sylveena, and her husband, the late Sammy Kowchai, to the Lord. He was very steep in a religious commitment that was deep in demonism for life. My late sister Sheila, one of my siblings joined the band. Mr. Edward Dookhan and his family were a great help to us in the early days. This village had hardly been touched with the Gospel. In 1967, we held a Crusade, and saw a number of converts. The church was formally established. Today, there is a functioning and growing church in the area.

I was joined by Winston Lynch who hailed from a neighboring village, Fort Wellington, and Oscar Motilall from the Corentyne. We held a number of crusades in No. 7 village, Cotton Tree, Bush Lot, Blairmont and a number of other villages along the coast. The late Evangelist Ramnarine was the main speaker and I was the Manager.

From Left to Right: Myself, Pastor Somai, Neville Solomon, Pastor Lynch and the late Bro. Persaud at the Cotton Tree Church

In each area, a church was planted after the crusade. From the No. 7 village church, another church was born in No. 5 village. This was in the 1970's. All these churches are growing and functioning for the glory of God, today.

One of the most powerful crusades was in Cotton Tree in 1969. I went and secured a plot of land. The owners were very kind to let us use it. In the first few nights of those thirty two nights of meetings we were the workers and the choir. By the third night, we drafted some young ladies from the Saine's family. They became a very integral part of the founding of this church. Many others were swept into the Kingdom of God. There were many healings and some got delivered from demon possession. There was one outstanding miracle that I could not forget. A mother brought an eight months old little baby. She told us that the baby at this age was not doing anything where movements were concerned. We prayed fervently. The next night, the mother testified that the baby began turning. The rest is history, God miraculously healed that child. Glory be to God. A few years later a plot of land was acquired and a beautiful building was erected during the times when Vivian Fredericks was the Pastor. Today, there is a vibrant, growing church. All praise to the King of Kings!

The fire of Evangelism and pioneering was burning in our bones. We went next to No. 7 village. Here again we saw a tremendous move of God. Evangelist Ramnarine was again the preacher. I was the Crusade Co-ordinator, and of course, the team of workers was bigger as there were now believers from Bath Settlement and Cotton Tree. We saw many born into the Kingdom of God. Many who are still serving God today in Guyana, and some in other countries of the world. A number of ministries have come forth from this church, Pastors Lokenath Ramkissoon, Herman Jacobs and his brother Jagat. We celebrate the Trophies of Grace, and the fact that a vibrant and functioning church is still in this area.

Like I have mentioned before, many outstanding Servants of God have come forth from these churches. To name a few, James Watts, Mahipaul, and Ovid Schultz, and many others over the past decades. No one ever imagined that these small beginnings would have produced results that have been making a Global Impact. It is very exciting to drive through these villages and not only see these churches but many other churches that are like brilliant torches to emanate the dynamic consequences of the Glorious Gospel. I must mention the late brother Prasad and his wife, sister Lily who made a very sterling and sacrificial contribution in the service of these churches.

I must note two families in Bush Lot that have stood out through the decades, the Raimal's and the Ramdat's. I am excited to announce a number of their children have been in ministry, and faithfully serving The Lord.

The Dynamism of Complementary Ministry

While the Fellowship and moreso, in this case, the Corentyne was impacted by Nationals and Locals, the Lord eventually brought us in contact with many other ministries over the years. Apostle Harry Das did not only have friends from the city come down to minister, but those from Trinidad, Canada and the USA. We had visitors all the way from India, sister Mamen, and brothers Chacko and Philip.

There was an outstanding and dynamic woman of God, Pastor Tenpow, who made many inputs in the early days of the work in the Corentyne. Today, my wife and I would constantly speak of how much we gained from the diversity of the ministries to which we were exposed. Our growth and stability in God can be attributed to this dynamism.

CHAPTER FOUR

THE TEAM FACTOR, CONNECTING WITH THE LATE APOSTLE PHILIP MOHABIR

Myself with the late Apostle Mohabir and his wife, Sis. Muriel

This was a very strategic and powerful ingredient that has been the life blood of the Full Gospel Fellowship. It was The Team Dynamic. I met Apostle Mohabir sometime in 1964. He preached at the church that used to meet by my home. He made such an impact on my life, that I remembered his message from Ephesians 4:1......"being a prisoner of the Lord." (KJV) That he preached, with great clarity and inspiration.

Together, they made a tremendous team, the Apostles Das and Mohabir. Apostle Mohabir was the visionary and strategist. He saw it and wanted to get it done now. Apostle Das wanted to wait on the Lord and water it with much prayers. The combination was surely extraordinary. That was why as full-blooded nationals they were able without any foreign help per se to found one of the most vibrant movements in the beautiful land of many waters called Guyana. At one time, many thought that Guyana would be the fountain head for the spread of Communism in this region, but God had spoken prophetically that our beautiful country would be the fountain head for the proclamation of the Gospel. I am so excited that I have lived long enough to see it happen. To God be the Glory!

I would not spend time to do a personal biography of Apostle Mohabir. He had ably and inexhaustively in his own scholatic style done it in his book, "Building Bridges." I want to spend some time to relate what I know about them working together.

Together, they labored with tremendous vision, mission and sacrifice. Together, they unselfishly and prophetically saw beyond their times and what few have perceived then. Together, they infused vision, zeal, faith and a God-given purpose in the lives of many young men and women whom they made to feel a sense of worth. Together, they took giant steps of faith to embark on missions that many would run from because of fear and lack of finances. Together, they founded what has been known as Full Gospel Fellowship of churches and ministers incorporated in 1968. So, let me endeavor to set the record straight by clearly stating that in my book, they were the co-founders of the Full Gospel Fellowship.

They were the Core of the Team. They were supported by a number of others, sister Muriel Mohabir, wife of the late Apostle Mohabir, the late Apostle Bryn Jones and his wife Edna, Missionary Ivor Hopkins, and Apostle Dennis Hilliman.

Bro. and Sis. Ivor and Clarine Hopkins

The late Apostle Bryn Jones and his wife, Edna with a group at Waterloo and Murray Streets (my sister Elsie on the top row extreme right)

They were also re-enforced by an army of young men and women whom they raised up.

While it was inevitably factual that Apostle Das was more involved in Berbice and Apostle Mohabir in Demerara and Essequibo, they were extremely supportive of each other and what was happening in the entire nation.

When Apostle Mohabir needed help in the Bible Training Center, he asked Apostle Das for me. That was how I got so integrally involved with Apostle Mohabir and the Training Center in 1969. He also became the key mentor in my life. He will always be missed by myself and family. My two daughters loved him.

When Apostle Das left Guyana in 1971, the task of running the Fellowship dropped in the lap of Apostle Mohabir. He ably did an indescribably sterling job. With the team of men and women he had, he did not only maintain what was there but pioneered new churches and even reached out to the Nations. Today, we must have missionaries in at least 30 countries around the world.

I will always remember the late Apostle Mohabir for his father's heart. This was so evident in his life and ministry that eventually and fondly he was called "Dad" by many and sister Muriel, his wife, mum. She is still so endearingly addressed by most.

The late Apostle Mohabir and his family in the early days

The late Apostle Mohabir did not only encourage and foster a spirit of team but also a spirit of family that was pregnated with a sense of love and care that engendered sharing. This surely fostered the team spirit. He would always tell the "workers," as we were called, that no matter where they were laboring that they belonged to a bigger team.

He was a man of undaunting faith, and a tremendous expositor of The Word. It was from him, I learnt how to read a verse or a portion of scripture over and over again, and glean points filled with truths.

He was very down to earth and very pragmatic, to the degree where a few felt he was sometimes sarcastic.

Farwell for the Mohabirs in 1983

CHAPTER FIVE
THE BIBLE TRAINING CENTER

Training of men and women for ministry was surely the heart beat of the late Apostle Mohabir. He would take insignificant lives and make some one out of them. I was fortunate to join a group of men whom Apostle Mohabir took to Essequibo for training. I believe that was the beginning of formal Training.

Brother Ivor Hopkins, from England, also taught during these months. I only spent three months. It was a life changing experience. The beach was sometimes our class room, and the sand our chalkboard. One of the first lessons I learnt on Bible Survey was through a diagram drawn on the sand by the late Apostle Mohabir. It was surely unforgettable. His burden for training was first to develop character. We were involved in evangelism and church planting. The churches in Hampton Court/Devonshire Castle; Henrietta and Red Lock were planted.

The Historic ......Stanleytown, West Bank Demerara

I was fortunate to be with the late Apostle Mohabir and team in 1965, when they went to have open air meetings to pioneer the church in this village. It was exciting and challenging to stand by the roadside next to the late Mr. Sackichand's store, singing, testifying and Preaching the Gospel. "Gospel shots were very popular during those times. Different ones will boldly quote a relevant verse of scripture. A nucleus of people, eventually responded to the Gospel. Meetings were held in a building owned by the late Mr. Chand. It was a real beautiful spot. It could have been described as romantic being situated by the banks of the majestic Demerara River. It was further enhanced by a concrete wall, which made it very scenic and very relaxing in the cool of the mornings and evenings in this tropical climate.

Myself with the late Cecil and Beno

This was a small and rather insignificant village where Full Gospel Fellowship had its early beginnings. The first church in this part of the country was founded here. It was here that some wonderful people were raised up for ministry. They are now impacting nations. There were some very outstanding and dedicated families, the Mangal's, the Armogan's, the Bruyning's, the Chand's, and the Ramlochan's. Brother Mangal, the late brothers David Armogan and Basil Kurrmiah with the late sister Bruyning were the first leadership team of the church.

It was here also that the Bible Training program took roots after the building was purchased, with a deposit in faith of just $400.00 (Guyana dollars). There were many mockers and critics surprisingly from other Ecclesiastical groups. They called us "cowboy preachers" and even "jokers." The late Apostle Mohabir simply replied, "We have no apologies for living by faith, then who will apologize for the Apostles of old, Peter and them?"

Group of Trainees – left to right: Cornelius, Mavis the late Vanessa and Andy

There were days when the trainees went with out food. There was no money. They were taught to give thanks for the empty plates and pray and believe God in anticipation for provision before the end of the day. I must relate one unforgettable incident. We had nothing to eat for breakfast. By the way, I was there serving as Assistant Principal to the late Apostle Mohabir from September 1969, and Pastor of the Stanleytown church. We met and gave thanks for nothing, but believed God for something. A sister from one of the neighboring churches who sold fruits and vegetables in the market came in that day with some fruits, exactly thirty two, one for each of us who were there. She was our miracle that day. It will take another book to relate all the testimonies of such happenings over these fifty years.

Stanleytown Church and the former Boys' Dormitory

Former Girls' Dormitory

More land was purchased and a dormitory for girls and staff was erected. By 1974, there were ninety four trainees. This was the largest number of Trainees ever. The late Apostle Mohabir preferred the concept of trainees to students, because the emphasis of his program was to develop character, more than just preparing to fulfill calling. So, training was not only in the classrooms but in the garden, in the Evangelistic outreach programs, in the maintenance of the property. It was the development of the whole person.

Myself with some of the faithful women of the Stanleytown Church

The First Camp – Sisters cooking for the Campers

Lionel Etwaru

Group of Campers at the First Camp in August 1966

Packed and ready to move from Stanleytown to Hauraruni

The Hauraruni Connection

Neville Solomon and Victor Raghunath, on behalf of the Guyana Youth Aflame, the Youth Arm of the Fellowship, undertook to apply for a plot of land from the Government for our youth camps. Hence, Hauraruni was secured in 1972. The Guyana Government leased to us a parcel of four hundred and sixty acres of land in the jungle along the Linden Highway. We began having Annual Youth Camps in very rugged conditions- with army tents, leaves on the ground covered with jute bags for sleeping. Baths were taken in the open by the Creek, toilets were just holes in the ground with walls made out of wood and leaves. The swarms of flies and the stench were sometimes unbearable in the tropical 85 degrees weather. The Lord did make up for these horrible conditions with his awesome presence in the meetings. Like Paul, the Apostle, I can say that His remarkable presence made the horrible conditions just a passing pain. Isn't HE always wonderful!

Dining Hall in Hauraruni

Dormitories in Hauraruni

Commendation was surely due to all those who ministered and served over the years in those conditions. The consequential results of lives transformed, and dozens responding to the Call of God for ministry can definitely be a source of encouragement and celebration. The Trophies of His Grace made it worthwhile.

For months, the late Apostle Mohabir and I talked and debated over moving the Training Center to Hauraruni. This was pressing because the facilities in Stanleytown were becoming over-crowded.

Finally, the date was set, March 5, 1975, and move impending. Suitcases, bags and boxes were packed. It finally came to pass when the trainees joined the "Launch" the ferry from Wales, West Bank Demerara to Grove, East Bank Demarara. The Exodus from Stanleytown to Hauraruni had begun. It was like the children of Israel crossing the Jordan. For us, it was a distant Canaan. We had to build it. This day of triumph was marked by a great tragedy. Elsie Dwarka, my sister, wife of Pastor David Dwarka, died in child birth. She was a woman of remarkable godliness and faith.

That fateful day, as the leader of this historic move, I had to cope with this deep pain and loss. I had to be the bearer of that news to my parents. They were devastated. She would always be remembered as a very special person by all who knew her. R.I.P my Beloved Sister!

My wife holding our eldest daughter, Kenise with a classroom in the background (Hauraruni)

Moving a band of over one hundred people with limited resources was a challenge in itself. There were no proper living quarters. We lived in canvas tents. We began to clear maiden forest with gigantic trees, vines and shrubs and many other unwelcome living creatures-- ants, snakes and tarantillas, to name a few. There was a bee-hive of activities-- designing buildings, clearing trees, cutting logs and peeling off the bark, making cement blocks and laying foundations became the program of those days. There were no classes for a few months. We only met for morning devotions and continued our week-end activities in the different churches to which we were designated.

Open Air Graduation

The dynamism of team-work became the hall mark of all those accomplishments. Teams were set up to clear the forest, build concrete blocks, prepare meals, peeling off the bark from logs, erecting the buildings, laying blocks etc. It seemed that the spirit of Nehemiah and his people pervaded the compound.

Today, those completed buildings speak for themselves. Whenever, I look at them, I struggle to accept that we did it. I am perpetually over-whelmed with a deep sense of gratitude to all those who labored arduously sometimes going beyond what was expected to have such a historic and remarkable accomplishment. To all the wonderful and willing people, I want to say a sincere "Thank You", and ask you to reflect and be proud of those days that caused you to accomplish such a herculean task. Be happy and proud that God allowed us to be there, "as such a time as that." Think of the teeming hundreds who have been blessed and affected for all time and eternity because of those facilities. If there has ever been any iota of doubt, frustration or feeling of wasted years, let my penning of these lines change your mind. Please see the bigger picture. You are an integral part of history in time and eternity.

I cannot close this chapter without honoring all who labored and I crave your indulgence to list some names. Honor must be given to the late Apostle Mohabir, not only to birth this vision but also daring to put action to see it come to pass. Sister Muriel Mohabir and the girls must be complimented for all their sacrifices. The late sister Violet Lewis, missionary from Jamaica who labored physically and spiritually. She must be honored for her contributions to the fulfillment of this vision. She also served as our Child Evangelism teacher. Her persistent intercessions, unwavering faith and support were pillars to this project. Bernice Morgan, who served as nurse, registrar and support not only to the women but the entire project. Elma Easton, a young woman who has given her life not only for physical work, but labored in the office and in deep intercessions and warfare. She still lives in Hauraruni and continues to make an exceptional and sterling contribution to the fulfillment of the total vision.

Keeshan and Mavis Banwarie have labored equally with all the others. He has arisen to be the mainstay until this day, not only as the Principal of the Training Center but overseeing the entire Hauraruni project. Such unwavering and undying commitment is rare in our times.

Deoram Timram and wife, trainee became graduate, pastor and leader today lives and teaches there. No one can ask for more commitment to the vision.

Andy Centano, who used the first power saw to cut any and everything in his way, labored unreservedly. He now lives and works for the Kingdom of God together with his wife, Ingrid, in Aruba.

Recognition and honor must also be attributed to the late Willam Bosveld from Holland for all his prayers and financial support from 1971 for our teachers, trainees and workers on the field.

The Guyana Missions in Sweden superceded them all. They did not only give financial support but became the back bone of support for the project in Hauraruni. They sent their own people to set up the Electricity system and the saw mill. They sent many containers with all kinds of stuff over the years. Too much to list.

I will put the Arubians in one block. They must be commended for their exceptional ability to adapt to labor that they were not accustomed to. I hope that they will appreciate that God has been honoring them over the years in things that they put their hands to do because of their willingness to serve in those difficult situations in that Season of their lives.

There is a list of names that I must also mention: Bethman Constantine, Elroyd Constantine, Patrick Fernandes, Awan Chatterpaul, Winston Lynch, James and Savitri Daniel from Trinidad, the late Patricia Greer from Trinidad, Barbara Fernandes, and many others. Too many to list in one book.

These were people who labored beyond the call of duty. It is very sad and dis-heartening that little is done to honor and recognize them in these times. Their dedication and hard work in the class room and on the project were an inspiration and encouragement to us as leaders.

Hence, the multi-faceted Hauraruni Establishment. Glory be to God!

First Kitchen in Hauraruni

Leaders' Conference in Hauraruni - 1989

CHAPTER SIX
THE INTERNATIONAL CONNECTIONS

The late Apostle Mohabir was a man of great faith and vision. From the very inception of Full Gospel Fellowship, he shared a very clear vision. He related that he saw many small candle lights glowing in the different Towns and Villages of Guyana. All were strategically set and growing in intensity and size. They grew larger and larger until they were connected and they became a great conflagration. He also saw these lights in the islands of the Caribbean, Suriname, French Guyana, Venezuela and Brazil, and beyond to the other continents.

The Full Gospel Fellowship was totally founded and built by nationals. But God eventually connected us with wonderful people in the Caribbean Islands and many other countries. To this day, we have great contacts in Trinidad. I have to list the Bhagoutie's, the Daniel's, Kenneth and Faith Ragoonath and the late Bertril Baird and Turnell Nelson. I have some personal friends, the Boodrams, Rafeeq and Irene Ali, Anthony Kawalsingh, Amar and Eutrice Rambissoon now in the USA, Ramnarine and Sue Maharaj also in the USA, the late Rampersaud and a number of other acquaintances. We have never founded a church in Trinidad because we felt that all our outstanding friends have been doing a great job. We were just complementing the fabulous work they were doing.

James and Savo Daniel and their daughter, Esther

Different ones of us from Guyana have had contacts, and ministered in other Islands. There was a fantastic connection that was made in St. Maarten. This started with Dennis Hilliman and Neville Solomon and was eventually established by Bishop Lewis Jones.

Apostle David Durant became the life link to Barbados where he went and pioneered a church that is flourishing and making an impact in the nation at large.

My wife and I ministering in Puerto Rico

The Founding of International Christian Leaders Connections

In 1990, Apostle Philip Mohabir invited a few key leaders who were working in different countries to a meeting in London. He said that there was a request and a call from many of our "Workers" in the nations who were expressing that they felt lonely and cut off. After some sessions of sharing how we can bridge this gap, we came up with this name and the purpose of "International Christian Leaders Connections.".……..**ICLC.**

I am so happy that I was there from the inception.

It was very clear that we were not setting up a denomination with some stringent structure that may bring more strictures, but fellowship founded on growing relationships.

It was concluded that this will be a means of expressing care through the dynamism of Relationships. This has been the cornerstone of all that God had enabled the late Apostle Philip Mohabir to build.

It should be a facilitator to create opportunity and help people find their places in the work of God.

That we should do everything possible to foster the vision and mission of reaching the nations.

The Aruban Connection

For me this is very special. It was my first mission trip outside of Guyana. In 1974, God sovereignly opened the doors to this beautiful, paradise island, universally known as,"One Happy Island." I always say that the Island, and moreso, the wonderful people have secured a very special place in my heart for life.

There was a tremendous move of God in the Island when we were invited to send someone. The late Apostle Mohabir and the then leadership team in Guyana decided that I should go. There was an actual revival in San Nicolas, the second city in the Island.

The late Bishop Ezra Williams and a team, from Harlem, New York City, USA, were on their way to Montserrat for a crusade. Their flight was diverted to the Island of Aruba because there was a storm in Montserrat. While they were stuck there, they got in contact with the Jackson Pentecostal Church. The Pastor was the late Pastor Connors. By this time, the church had about six elderly but extremely faithful people. I was told that for years, these ardent believers, would religiously open the doors of the church and attend every meeting that they should have during the week.

A crusade ensued. It was led by the late Bishop Williams and team. About two hundred souls got saved and came into the Kingdom of God. Among these converts were dozens of young people. The team was not really prepared for such a move. Deacon Arthur Cudjoe and his brother Alvin were left to help the new converts. They did a tremendous job to hold it together. But, they desired to see more growth and development in these young converts.

Then, God orchestrated another Providential move. Bernice Morgan, who moved to Guyana from England to work with the late Apostle Mohabir, visited Aruba during this time. She was then the nurse at the Training Center. She was ill and went to recuperate as her family was living in the Island. She ended up in the English speaking church in San Nicolas. She saw the need for more ministry, and unhesitantly contacted Guyana. The lot fell on me to answer this seeming Macedonian call. I did not even have a passport, and in those days travelling from Guyana was almost like a nightmare because of the documents that were needed. Anyway, it took me about three weeks to make all plans and get all my documents. That was a miracle!

I arrived in Aruba to find a life changing and historic challenge. I ministered with unswerving zeal and enthusiasm for fourteen consecutive nights. I had classes every morning from 10.00 am to 12.00 noon in the mission home. The hunger for the Word of God and His ways was almost indescribable. Many received the Baptism of the Holy Spirit. The greatest highlight was fourteen of the young people responded to the call of God for ministry.

They eventually ended up in the Bible Training Center in Guyana. They were namely, Gilbert Maartes, Thomasito Gibbs, Castello, Victoria Gibbs, George Riley, Pedro Arindell, Marva Cyrus, Betty Baptiste, Glenda Doncker, the late Frederick Hempstadt, Marilyn, Joan Maartes, Leonardo and Mauricio Hazel. They left everything and went to Guyana for three years. Those days must have been some of the most difficult times economically and politically in Guyana. If they did not enjoy it all, they surely did an excellent job to endure it with flying colors. Today, we can celebrate the Goodness and Greatness of God upon their lives. A number of them have really grown and developed in their ministries. They have pioneered churches and have been leading them in Aruba and other countries.

My wife and I with Marva (far left) and Glenda (far right)

Apostle/Pastor Gilbert Maartes has pioneered and been pastoring a growing and vibrant church in Aruba. He is supported by his wife, Pastor Stella and his daughters and a team of wonderful men and women who are in the leadership. He also leads the organization of pastors, APU…..Aruba Pastors Union. He has also been ministering in many other countries.

July 2013 - My wife and I with Pastor Gilbert and his wife, Stella

Apostle/Pastor Thomasito Gibbs and wife, Pastor Victoria have been leading the church in San Nicolas, now" Seed of Life Ministries," where it all began. They now have built a majestic building to house the church. The mission home is still standing as an evident mark of historical significance. They have been taking teams to other countries to perpetuate the proclamation of the gospel.

The late Apostle/Pastor Frederick Hempstadt and his late wife, Pastor Patricia who hailed from Trinidad, and was also trained in

Guyana, pioneered a Papimento speaking church in San Nicolas. This church is now led by their daughter, Pastor Tabitha Hempstadt and husband, with a faithful team of leaders.

Pastor Glenda Doncker and her husband, Dr./Pastor Orlando Wilson are laboring in a church they have pioneered in St Maarten. They also work with other ministries on the island and take teams to minister in other countries.

We celebrate the others who may not be leading churches, but who continue to serve God, and are faithfully involved in diverse ministries in the churches where they are.

They are definitely listed as Trophies of the immeasurable Grace of God.

Joan Maartes who was married to the late Pastor Lawrence Eccles, has taken the challenge to pastor and lead the church in Curacao. We applaud her and all the leaders who are supporting her for the expansion of the Kingdom of God.

This Aruban Connection has also brought us in contact with a number of other ministries in Aruba; the church that was started by Eric and Clementine Alberga; Apostle/Pastor Arno and Lois; Pastor/Dr.Taio and Nelly Orman de Cuba; Pastor Andy Centano, and his wife, Ingrid.

This connection brought us into relationship with some wonderful folks in Curacao. Kenneth and Enika Thym were our first contacts. Then, eventually the late Lawrence Eccles. Both churches with outreaches are still growing and glowing as they work to fulfil the great commission.

First set of Arubans heading to the Bible Training Center in 1974

My wife and I visiting Aruba in 1990

The St. Maarten (the Friendly Island) Connection

From Aruba, I went to St.Maarten, where Neville Solomon was pastoring the church founded in Philipsburg, by Dennis Hilliman. At that time, he was constructing the church building. I spent one week with him. Every morning we went and worked on the building. The late Jimmy Edwards and Cornelius Rabess were also involved in the construction. We went home by 1:00 pm, had lunch, rested and then went in the evening to evangelize by holding open air meetings. I remembered us holding a meeting on the French Side. By the time, I was ready to speak the cops came and shut us down as we had no permit. As a result of this trip, the late Jimmy Edwards, Cornelius Rabess, and Rita Brooks responded to the call of God and went to Guyana to study. Later, they were joined by Harold Richardson, Uriel and a few others.

February 2014 - My wife and I with Rita and Pedro – Graduates from Hauraruni

Today, Pastor Rita Edwards, wife of the late Jimmy Edwards, whom he found in Guyana, is pastoring the church they pioneered a few years ago, on the French side. How about that? Rita brooks, who is now Rita Richardson is still serving the Lord and is a recognized Gospel singer. Harold Richardson, and his wife, Yvonne, who hails from Guyana are very much involved in the church where they are members. Cornelius Rabess and his wife, Hazel, of Guyanese descent, are servants of God serving Him at large. They now reside in Florida, USA.

The next leg of my trip took me to Trinidad, the land of the steel pan and the humming bird. I was hosted by Pastor Walter Bhagoutie and family. This was a very restful time from the prior hectic weeks. I was able to make contact with the Daniel's family, and Rafeeq and Irene Ali. James and Savitri Daniel made the bold decision to pursue ministry and headed to Guyana to be trained at the Bible Training Center. They made a great sacrifice to leave everything, their possessions and children as they moved to Guyana. I am sure that in spite of all the struggles and privations over the years, they can celebrate the goodness of God upon their lives and those of their children. They were able to pioneer a vibrant church that is still growing in Trinidad. Today, they continue to serve God and are involved in many ways in Kingdom business.

Many Caribbean Islands were impacted by this prophetic move of God. The wonderful thing was that students came from them to study in the Bible Training Center in Guyana, which God said will be the fountain head for the proclamation of the Gospel in this Region.

February 2014 - My wife and I with Pastors Orlando and Glenda

The Venezuelan Connection

In the midst of all the migration from Guyana during the mid 1970's and 1980's, there were many christians and pastors who were part of those numbers. It was amazing how people were desperate to leave Guyana because of all the political and economical privations. Many ended up in countries like Suriname. French Guiana, Brazil and Venezuela with different cultures and languages. We have quickly learnt that God had a bigger plan for us, a seemingly insignificant people to reach the nations.

My wife and I with the Pastors in Venezuela

I was amazed to learn that tens of thousands of our people crossed the border to Venezuela. Among these immigrants, there was one outstanding family, the Kurmiah's. The late Basil Kurmiah was an elder in the first church that the late Apostle Philip Mohabir pioneered in Stanleytown, West Bank Demerara. He was very zealous for God, and had a burning burden to reach men and women with the Gospel. He, immediately and unhesitantly began to evangelize in that part of Venezuela. Most of his children and his wife joined him to pioneer a church. One of his daughters Mavis and her husband, Errol are the key leaders in the group of some faithful pastors and other workers. They, now have at least five churches in the San Felix and Puerto Ordaz areas.

It was my honor, to visit with them a few times and make some ministry inputs.

These wonderful people are indeed Trophies of His Amazing Grace!

How else can we describe it? One man had a Vision and was faithful to pass it on to others, Empowering them to Envision and Empower others to Impact nations, and fulfill the Great Commission.

Myself and Pastor James Daniel – my first Missions Trip to Venezuela

The African Connection

The late Apostle Mohabir had some contacts in Nigeria and a few other African nations. He even made trips to Nigeria to minister. But, it was the Apostle Harry Das who ripped open the African continent. After more than thirty years, he had reached into at least ten African countries, plus India, England and a number of other nations. He has been able to raise a substantial army of dedicated missionaries who are promulgating the growth and expansion of the hundreds of churches. I feel that Kenya must be recognized as the base with the strongest and most formidable work. His Annual Conference in Nairobi would easily draw about fifteen thousand attendees. I have had the opportunity to be in one of these conferences when they celebrated their twenty fifth anniversary. It was quite an awesome experience.

In 1998, the Lord providentially brought me in contact with two dynamic servants of God from South Africa. They were Bishops Sammy Musepa and Solly Lallamani. Both have pioneered and been pastoring two thriving churches in Pretoria. They have also been reaching out to other African countries---- Nigeria, Zambia, Zimbabwe, Namibia and the Congo. I was able to visit with them the same year and God has forged a terrific relationship between us. One that has enabled us to be involved in Annual Conferences and even to travel and minister in the other nations. We even embarked on a Bible School in the city of Rustenburg for about three years. That is no longer functioning. But it must be noted that the first batch of graduates are all involved in ministry. A few are pastors and one has been serving as the Dean of a Bible School in that same city.

I must mention an another outstanding Apostle and Servant of God, Winston Lynch. He also went to Africa in the mid- seventies and worked with Apostle Harry Das for a few years. He then started his own Fellowship of Churches in a number of African countries. We celebrate the commitment and dedication that have been shown by him, his wife Shirley and family. He spends more time in Africa than in a Charlotte, North Carolina, USA, where he now resides. Trophies of Grace for which we give Glory to the of the Harvest.

First set of Students in the Bible School – Rustenburg, South Africa

Fabulous Trophies of Grace for the Glory of King Jesus!

Connections and lively relationships have been established with a number of other outstanding servants of God. In the city that my friend calls, "God's country" the magnificent Cape Town, is the amazing Apostle Kobus Swartant and his wonderful wife Hazel. In Durban, there are a few great contacts, Dr. Randlee and a few others.

Winston Lynch with his wife, Shirley and Family standing at the back with Doris on the extreme Right. Herman and Janice sitting in front.

From left to right: Apostle Sammy, myself,
Bishop Solly and the late Walter – 1998

Also in Johannesburg, Evangelist/ Pastor Joseph Kansema; and Dr./ Bishop David Lazarus have been great contacts.

November 2013 - My wife and I with Dr. Sammy –
Conference in Pretoria, South Africa

THE TROPHIES OF GRACE

November 2013 - My wife and I with Pastor Chris and his wife – Rustenburg, South Africa

My wife and I with Apostle Hauna Goroh – Namibia, 2012

The Asian Connection

Ministering in Conference – Bhopal, India

For years, the late Apostle Mohabir had been in touch with Apostle Vachan Bhandari. He is still one of the outstanding men who with his family have been planting churches and running schools through which he presents the Gospel. Dr. Samuel Matthai and his wife have returned to India, after living twenty five years in the USA. He has been equipping men and women in his Bible School and sending them out from the base in the City of Bhopal to other cities in India to plant churches. In Chennai, I have a long standing friend and honorable servant of God, Pastor Victor, who has pioneered and been pastoring a growing church. I have had the privilege to visit and minister in Tiruwalla, South India with Bishop Thomas Philip. In that area, I have been in relationship with Bishop Mathai. I am yet to visit him and his work. I was able to visit with Apostle Samuel Francis in Bhopal and have thoroughly been blessed with the tremendous work he is doing in that city and others. In Bombay, it has been such a blessing to be working with Brother Gladstone and his wife Priscilla. It is overwhelming to see the blessings of God in their ministry as they plant churches and run a home to rescue boys and girls from the treacherous streets of Bombay. It has also been a privilege to relate with the vibrant ministry of Bishop D.C Kaushal in Delhi.

Pastor Gladstone and his wife - Bombay, india

Myself with Apostle James Cooper and Biship
Thomas Philip – Tiruwalla, India

Myself with Apostle Vachan Bhandari and his wife – Dehra Dun, India

Then in the late 1990's, there was a great connection with two key brothers in Malaysia, Apostles David Ramayiah and Alan Tan and their wives. My wife and I had the opportunity to visit once in 2003, and minister in the churches. This trip was the fulfillment of a dream my wife had in 1973. This dream added to the confirmation of us getting married, as she saw me accompanying her on a mission trip to Malaysia, long before I even proposed to her. We will always remember the openness and great unreserved expression of hospitality by the pastors and the believers.

These brothers have been reaching to North Vietnam, Thailand and Myanmar. The vision just keep expanding and the Trophies for the King of kings constantly increasing. There will be an innumerable number that no man can count. Glory be to God!!!!

Ministering in the church of Apostle Alan Tan – Malaysia

The Suriname & French Guyana Connection

Apostle Mohabir marked in red these neighboring countries on the original map, when he shared the Vision. From Guyana, we did not pioneer churches, as such in these countries, but God had sovereignly connected us with Apostle James and sister Linda Cooper in 1965. They have been instrumental in pioneering over thirty churches in Suriname, and raising up dozens of workers over the past four decades. It is amazing how God has used trying economic and political times to disperse his people, and expand the Kingdom. Many Surinamers migrated to French Guiana; hence a number of churches have been established there also. Note has to be taken that from Guyana, we have sent a few missionaries over the years to Suriname. The late Kedlall Jhugdeo and his dear wife, Joyce must have been the first. They were followed by Evangelist Harry Outar and his wife Anjanie. They are still living and pastoring there. Apostle Elsworth Williams spent a few years there also.

Sherlock and Mavis Tacoordeen have also been in Suriname for many years. He is pastoring a church just outside of the city of Paramaribo.

The connection has ever been strong, and it keeps getting stronger.

Sherlock and Family – Missionaries to Suriname

The European Connection

The late Apostle Mohabir also opened the doors to Europe, especially in England, the Scandinavian countries and Holland. He himself had spent many years living, ministering and pioneering churches in England and Sweden before he returned to Guyana in 1964. He, actually went back to England in 1983, and labored there until the Lord called him home.

From Holland, the late William Bosveld had financially supported many missionaries and projects in Guyana since 1971. I had the privilege, over the period of many years, to visit with him and his family and minister in many churches, that supported the World-Wide Mission, in Holland, Germany, Denmark and Norway. Through the contacts of the late Apostle Mohabir, I also travelled and ministered in many churches in Sweden and Finland. They have been supporting the Fellowship since the 1960's. Mention must be made of two main players, the late Hilding Fagerburg and Albert Swenson, among the many others, who are still in contact with Guyana, and seek to be all the support that they can.

Preaching in Missions Conference – Holland

Preaching in Denmark with Pastor Allan Hansen

The North American Connection

During the 1970's and 1980's and ever since, tens of thousands of Guyanese migrated to Canada and the United States, particularly New York City. Among this multitude of Guyanese has been many Christians and Pastors from Full Gospel Fellowship and many other groups. At first, there was a kind of condemnative attitude to these folks. Then, we began to realize that God was expanding our borders in a non conventional way. So, we began to work to gather these believers. Hence, a number of churches mushroomed in New York City, Toronto and other states wherever the Diaspora went.

Today, there are churches in New York City, Schenectady, Fort Lauderdale, Orlando, Washington D.C, New Port News and Richmond in Virginia just to name a few. Where there has not been a gathering of the believers, pastors have been leading churches in many states in the USA. Joshua and Becky Persaud have pioneered and been pastoring a church in Fort Lauderdale, Florida. Seeram and Karla Garney are pastoring a church, which they have pioneered in Alton, Illinois. Seeram came from the church in Fyrish, Corentyne. Lloyd and Barbara Sewdin have pastored in a number of cities in the USA, and now they are in Ogden Dunes, Indiana.

Pastor Dexter Singh, his wife Chandra and family reside in Little Falls, Minnesota where they Pastor a growing church. Both him and his wife are trophies of Grace from the Corentyne.

I also got caught up in this migration fever. God did a miracle for my family and I. A member of a church in Berwick, Louisiana, sister Gerrie Breaux, spoke with a congressman in 1985, about the difficulty for me to be able to take the children with us when we travel to the USA. He called the US Embassy in Guyana, and within a few months, we were issued Resident Visas. The whole family began travelling once per year and then we finally decided to move permanently in August 1989.

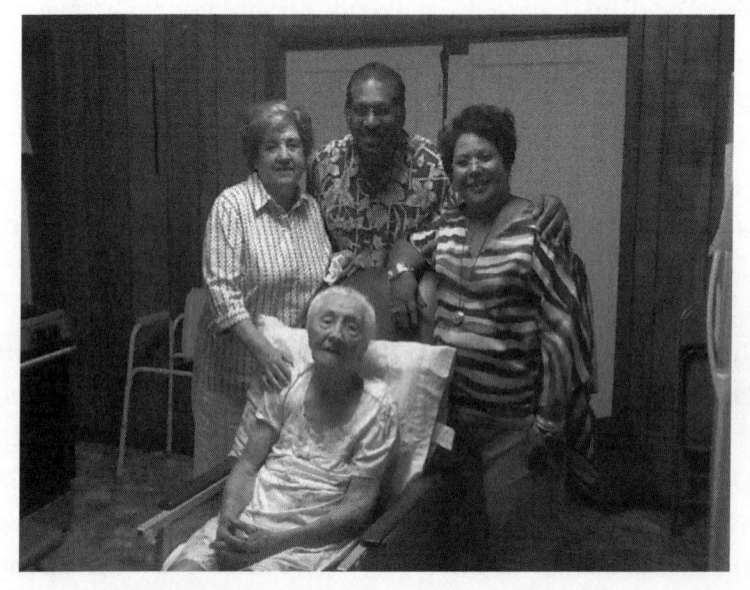

Myself and wife with Gerrie Breaux and Pastor Toot Drikill (sitting) – Berwick, Louisiana - 2013

We started in Hickory, North Carolina, moved to Newark, Delaware for three years and then finally to Holbrook, Long Island. During this time, we started the church in Richmond Hill, Queens. The church commenced in the basement of the home of brother and sister Harry Samaroo at 124th street in Richmond Hill. Brother Chetram Samaroo, with Pastor Ramkissoon mobilized the brethren in the beginning. We outgrew the basement and moved to the YMCA on Parsons Blvd. for some time, then to another church in Queens Village. We even rented a room at a Knights of Columbus for a period before we rented a store front. Eventually, we bought our own building on 97-02 Jamaica Ave. in Woodhaven, New York.

My wife cutting the ribbon for the dedication of
the 97-02 Jamaica Ave. Church Building

The church continued to grow from 1993 to November 2008 when we purchased the historic and architecturally designed gothic building on 86-02, 115th street in Richmond Hill.

Present Church Building

Myself and wife in front of our present Church Building – 2014

Our Fellowship Hall

This did not stop us from travelling to many countries ministering in leaders conferences, conventions, marriage enrichment forums and youth camps. This was the main purpose for our move to the USA, that we will use it as a spring board to travel to the nations. The other reason was my children's education.

Today, our eldest daughter, Kenise is the head of a Human Resources department for a large non profit organization that rebuilds the lives of homeless and previously incarcerated men in New York City, New Jersey and Philadelphia. In addition, she is very much involved in ministry at our local church. She serves as the Minister of Praise and Worship, along with being instrumental in working with the Singles and Youth ministry teams. Kenise has a 4 year old daughter, Aviah (our first grandchild).

Kenise leading Praise and Worship

Aviah Elizabeth – Kenise's Daughter (4 years old)

Delene, our younger daughter, has finished her Residency as a Pediatrician/Internist in June 2013. She now lives in Cincinnati,

Ohio, where her husband Matthew is doing his final year of Residency in Surgery.

Delene and her husband, Matthew on their wedding day – February 2009

The Brazilian Connection

Awan Chatterpaul, who was converted from Hinduism, in No. 56 village, Corentyne, and was trained at the Bible Training Center in Hauraruni went to Brazil in 1995. He has definitely bought the vision shared by the late Apostle Mohabir, that the lights will go beyond the borders of Guyana. In fact, just before the Lord promoted the Apostle to Glory, the last light was ignited in the Lethem area bordering Guyana and Brazil in the south.

Awan testified that he went beyond the border to Brazil, just touching the tip of this enormous country. He started out in Lethem, but pushed into Brazil to look for the families who were connected to those in the Lethem area. He hoped to further spread the vision. It took him about five years to work his way into the tribes. He needed this time to befriend them, earn their trust and learn the language. During these years many meaningful relationships were established that contributed to the foundation that had been laid.

The Brazilian ministry got off the ground in the year 2000. It was registered with the Federal Government as a Charitable Organization in 2001, by the name " Missao Evangelica Sem Fronterias"...... .."Evangelistic Mission Without Borders." There are Five Facets to this ministry: 1. Ministry to the Amerindians in the jungle areas. 2. Ministry to the people in the city. 3. Ministry among the street children. 4. Small scale socio-economical development. 5. Training Center for youths.

Through this ministry, he has been able to reach Nine different tribes. So far they have planted Eighty Seven churches. All of them have their own Leadership, and functioning autonomously. In the city of Boa Vista, there are Four churches with their own buildings. They are debt free. They have a feeding program where at least one hundred children are fed each week. They also run a school with about Eighty Five children who cannot afford to go to the Government Schools.

There are a number of projects that are functioning to enable the people to be self sufficient. The Training Center has thirty five students drawn from Eight different nations. The Vision is to move into other areas and reproduce the vision.

What a celebration of all these Trophies of Grace for Our Wonderful Savior.

The Pakistan Connection

I have always carried a burden since 1982 for the Muslim nations. Much has not happened for me to go to anyone as yet. But the Lord has brought me in contact over the past five years with some Pastors in Karachi and Faisalabad. I am hoping that in October of 2014, I will be able to visit with them and their churches. I have been preaching by phone almost every Friday and some Sundays in their services in Karachi. Plus we are working with them to complete their church building.

CHAPTER SEVEN
THE UNKNOWNS (SOME UNSUNG HEROES)

I have deliberately chosen to include this chapter because I feel that this is a very special time in our history, Fifty Years Anniversary. I am not too sure how many of us will be here for the 100 years Anniversary. So, I feel that this is the time to recognize these outstanding people. Apostle James Cooper always say that to every soldier on the frontline, there is a group of eighteen allocated to his support. So, there are always people who work in the background to make things happen, and we sometimes only hail those in the forefront. Of course, every one cannot be number one. This Fellowship can celebrate 50 years because of the dynamism of the team spirit that was always perpetuated by many dedicated men and women over the years. Of course, I have often said that Heaven has perfect records that no one can dispute. That is what matters in the end!

I do hope that this Baton will continue to be passed on!!

Nehemiah, has been one of my favorite characters in the Bible. The more I share about him and his accomplishments, the more I realize that there was a long list of Unknowns, who made a sterling contribution, only their names were not mentioned. But they were just as important as those in the fore.

Hence, as I thought about this book and drew up my plan, I convinced myself that my work will be incomplete if I do not give time and space for the teeming list of Unknowns. I am even struggling where to begin, but like everything, I must begin somewhere. When Apostle Das went to the Corentyne, he came with a small team. Dennis Hilliman was part of the team. He was a support ministry who made a tremendous impact alongside the Apostle. His strong teaching and prophetic ministry touched many. I cannot forget his impact on my life. He was the first person who prophesied over me about the call and hand of God upon my life. He also prayed with me and a few others to be baptized with the Holy Spirit at Waterloo and Murray Streets in Georgetown in 1965. Brothers Joshua John and De'abrew also helped in those early days in the Corentyne with the music, playing the guitar and accordion, respectively. There were no elaborate music bands, but these few instruments with some tamborines, and much clapping of hands. The hands were called the "ten stringed instrument." This was one of the reasons we were mockingly called the "clap hand church."

I have to list the late sister Lily Prasad, a sister of Apostle Das. She was a woman of great faith and intercession, who undauntingly and sacrificially supported her brother, and served with unswerving commitment in those trying early days in the mid-1960's. She was an outstanding personal evangelist, and excellent with new believers. I do remember how she came to my home and patiently precept upon precept taught my mom and dad as young believers. I used to take her on a bicycle for more than one mile to meetings in Chesney. She taught me how to call the words of a song, as the group sang, because of the limited song books. I cannot forget those favorite hymns that were so inspirational in those days; " What a Friend we have in Jesus" "I Surrender All" " Draw Me Nearer" " At The Cross" " Redeemed how I love to Proclaim it" " He Took My Sins Away" and numerous others. Too many to mention here. These were followed by some very lively choruses, "Cushi, Cushi, Mano." " I Looked up the Road and I Wondered." "Jesus Took my Burdens," "Oh, Howl Love Jesus," and many more. Of course, in these times, they tell me that they do not sing "hims" (hymns) any more, they only sing "hers." (Choruses).

Another gentleman who labored in the Corentyne, and was the pastor of the main church in Rose Hall for a period, was the late Reverend Harry Binda. I always remembered how the Lord used him in an extraordinary way for a period of time. He could never finish a sermon, God would just interrupt the meeting and folks will be getting healed, delivered and filled with the Holy Spirit. Those were amazing times. The meetings were unpredictable but very exciting and pregnated with the Presence of the Lord.

The Lord did not only use and bless the Nationals, but He graciously and with great Prophetic purpose, connected us with ministries from abroad. We had the honor of receiving the youthful and late Brother Bryn Jones and his wife Edna from England. He was an outstanding Evangelist/Pastor. He was my pastor in the Corentyne for one year. He worked with Apostles Das and Mohabir to draw up the Constitution to register theF ull Gospel Fellowship in 1968. He ministered throughout Guyana before he returned to England after a few years. He became one of the pioneers of the Apostolic move of God in England in the 1980's, and was leading one of the streams until the Lord called him home.

In Guyana, he worked contemporaneously with Brother Ivor Hopkins, also from England. Brother Ivor Hopkins served in many areas in Guyana, but the longest in the Corentyne, where he found his darling bride Clarine Bhajan. Both of these people made an indelible impact on my life. He was a blessing with his outstanding teaching ministry. I boast that I still use his notes on the doctrine of God from 1967. Clarine was a school teacher and a very hard worker in the church. She helped me as a student and a young believer. Today they live in England with a beautiful family, and are still ministering.

There were missionaries from Trinidad who contributed to the work, especially in the Corentyne. The late brother and sister Stansky, Evangelist Ramkissoon, Rampersaud and Turnell Nelson, with Bertrill Baird. A number of ministries came from Canada and the USA. I have to list the Lawrenson's from Canada. There were even missionaries from South India, sister Mammen, a tremendous teacher who spent a prolonged period in the Corentyne. She was a great blessing in those early pioneering days. Dr. Chacko and brother Philip were amazing preachers who released their uninhibited gifts in dividing the unadulterated Word of God. I remember Dr. Chacko sharing on Israel, being the war-weapon of God, and the place of Israel in the Last Days Program of God.

It did not take long for us to realize that God was connecting us with all these people in different nations to fulfill His initial Vision to us as a Fellowship. What vision? To reach the lost in our country, plant churches, raise up laborers to reach our nation and the nations of the world. Can I mention, that I am so excited and overwhelmed that I have lived long enough to see that fulfilled to the letter. I have seen men and women saved and trained in Guyana from ordinary beginnings accomplishing extraordinary things around the world. This began to happen at a time, when Guyana was rivaling Haiti for the top spot to be the poorest nation in the Western Hemisphere. What an amazing God, we serve!! Besides Him, there is No Other God!

It is difficult to imagine, without God, what accomplishments could have been achieved to fulfill purpose and destiny. Today, after 50 years, we have over 120 churches in Guyana, missionaries in about 30 nations, and the only Full-Time Bible School.

Many of us are impacting nations in evangelism, planting churches and reproducing leaders to perpetuate the expansion of the Kingdom of God.

First Office and Mission Home in South Road

The late Kedlall Jhugdeo and his wife Joyce were the first missionaries who were sent out to Suriname to work with Apostle James Cooper. He also became the first pastor of the Church in South Road, Georgetown. He must be listed as our first missionary to India. Presently, his dear wife and children are living in North Carolina, and they continue to serve the Lord.

From left to right: Myself, the late Kedlall Jhugdeo with 2 of his friends and the late Beno

The late Sydney Bygrave, who was born in Jamaica and migrated to Canada, also served in Guyana for many years. He was a great teacher/pastor, and encourager of the brethren. I had the honor to have him work with me when I pastored the church in Stanleytown in the early 1970's.

The late Brother Cline from the Bronx, New York City, 1964-1966, made a tremendous impact with his dynamic teaching and intercession gifts while we were at Waterloo and Murray streets.

Lloyd Sewdin, another product of the ministry of the Apostle Das. Prior to his leaving Guyana in 1971 to study, in Jamaica and then the USA, he held many crusades and pastored in the Corentyne. He has always been an anointed and outstanding Evangelist. On his return to Guyana in 1975, he made a tremendous impact across the country as he released his Evangelistic gifting. His first crusade was held in Rose Hall Town. During those five nights of meetings, many got saved, healed and delivered from demonic possession. I remember one night that 32 persons were screaming, jumping and rolling on the floor as demons began to manifest. It was great to see them gloriously delivered. From these meetings, a church about 10 miles away, in the village of Cromarty was born. We baptized 137 converts in one day, at the no. 63 beach, as a result of these meetings. That must have been the largest number of people ever baptized in one day. The same outstanding results were reported as he travelled across the country and ministered in Linden, Georgetown, Stanleytown and Essequibo. The church in Kwakwani was established after a crusade with him that I managed.

Evangelist Lloyd Sewdin, wife Barbara and daughter, Ashley

There are some people from the Corentyne that I must mention. The late Seodat Satdeo, who pastored and pioneered churches until the Lord called him home. His wife, sister Mary is still involved in the church in no. 35 village.

Vishnu Shiwpal, also labored in those early days of great need and privations in the Corentyne. He rode his bicycle covering many miles as he served. He was pastor of the church in Rose Hall. He now resides in the USA with his family. He has also pastored churches in the USA.

He was succeeded by Margaret Sewdin, who is now Margaret Etwaru. She served until 1977, when we got married. She moved with me to live and work in Hauraruni while we pastored the church in Stanleytown. Then in 1979, when Kenise, our first child was born, we were asked to go back to the Corentyne where we served until we migrated to the USA in August 1989.

Badri and Peter Persaud, and their sister Margaret, also served with their late mom and their other siblings in this thriving work in the Corentyne. The late brother Persaud, their dad also served in many projects. They rode bicycles then motor cycles for many miles to attend church in Rose Hall and to be involved in a number of other activities. They, eventually, migrated to Canada where they helped to pioneer a church with a few others, Emmanuel and Enid Mendonca, David and Kema Dwarka and Sherlock Singh. The two brothers now live in the USA. Badri has served as a leader in a church in Virginia, and Peter is actually working from the church in Fort Lauderdale to pioneer another church with a few other brethren.

Oscar Motilall who hails from the Corentyne and labored with me in West Coast Berbice, where he found his bride, Joyce, is now pastoring a church in West Virginia.

Note must be taken of a flaming Evangelist, Michael Patterson, whose ministry made a tremendous impact on radio throughout Guyana. He was the pioneer of the church in Albouystown. A church that is moving with great power in this area under the leadership of Apostle Elsworth Williams.

David Tomlinson and Dennis Marshall from England with a few others who were sent by the late Apostle Bryn Jones at the request of the late Apostle Mohabir, brought some great complementary insights and prophetic inputs at a very crucial time in the Fellowship between 1978 and 1983. They contributed to help us break through some ceiling areas that catapulted the work to another dimension.

Once again, we proved the dynamism of complementary ministry.

CHAPTER EIGHT
THE LESSONS

I feel that I will not do justice to this book, if I do not cite a list of lessons I have learnt, and the which I would like to note in an effort to pass them on to the Next Generations.

1. It is the little nuggets and more so the basics that make us effective and efficient and bring longevity to what we become and do for God. This is what we share with believers, Life of prayer, Reading and learning the Word of God, Fellowship with the saints, Sharing my faith with diligence, Living as if the Lord would Return Today!
2. Understanding that God has a Plan for my life. I need to find that plan. I need to find my place and function therein. Remember, God *sets* us in the body. 1 Corinthians 12: 8, 28.
3. Be connected to a Team. The devil fights and works to destroy Relationships at all levels. He vehemently and mercilessly targets Loners.
4. Find where God has planted you, thrive and flourish in fruit-bearing there. Do not run around or be a cruise-matic Christian.
5. I always remember some of the little nuggets that my mentor, the late Apostle Philip Mohabir passed on. He would always

say, " You are not qualified to lead, unless you are willing to be led." It will be very revealing to ask some leaders who leads them.

"You must never be found alone in a room with a woman, unless she is your mother or your wife."

"Listen more, speak less, that is why God gave us one mouth and two ears."

"Always guard yourself against the three "G's" ……..Gold, Gals and Glory."

6. " Stay low" the devil cannot easily hit you when you are low. That's why we often see in battles in movies, soldiers trying to stay low in gun fire.
7. For pastors; " take care first of your number one sheep, your wife. Her condition will tell you the condition of the other sheep in the fold."
8. The need of having a mentor, at least one person with whom you can share your innermost feelings and thoughts.
9. Titles, were a secondary thing, maybe in those days we were guilty of playing it down, but, I tell you what, the production of fruits was undeniably evident. Souls were being born in the Kingdom, genuine conversions, demons casted out and people being set free, churches being birthed in villages thought impossible to penetrate with the Gospel. After fifty years, there is no doubt that God has vindicated His Word and His Servants.

Of course in these days, there seems to be a special gift and ministry that gives heavy titles to anyone who preaches a little and have a few followers. I never forget in one of my travels a young man greeted me and introduced himself as Apostle so and so. I, in my peculiar way, asked what was he apostleing. He said to me that he had a church with about six people.

10. It was emphasized that when you enter a new area that the Prince demon needed to be identified and that you bind the strong man then spoil his goods.
11. "You do good, you do for your self; you do bad, you do for yourself." Apostle Harry Das. He preached one of his typical sermons in the church that Sunday that was about two hours long on this thought.
12. No one man, no single group can get this job done. We have to do it together. We need to remember that in the Bible we see the power of Unity. The two significant times: the Tower of Babel and Pentecost.
13. You cannot take people higher than where you are yourself.
14. People will never care how much you know until they know how much you care.
15. One thing is Constant: change. Change is inevitable, not to change is a sure sign of imminent extinction. Motto: "CONSTANT CHANGE IS HERE TO STAY."
16. "There is no more powerful engine driving an organization toward excellence and long-range success than an attractive, worthwhile, and achievable Vision for the future, widely shared" ………Burt Nanus (Visionary Leadership, 1992:3)
17. The Dynamism of being the Second Man. I will have to do another book just to cover this subject. It was my honor to serve both of my leaders. I definitely spent a lot more years and got closer to the late Apostle Mohabir and his immediate and extended family. Much of what I am, and have accomplished to this day, can be attributed to the time I have spent, served and worked alongside him. I was willing to be the Timothy. In fact, when I told him that one evening

as we were fellowshipping, he said to me, "Lio. You think very highly of yourself." I thought that I was honoring him, by telling him I felt like Timothy sitting at the feet of Paul the Apostle.

18. "Never let limited Finances determine the pursuit of a Vision God has given you." (Apostle Philip Mohabir) God is able to give the "Pro-vision.
19. My mentor always emphasized; Character must equal Calling: Messenger must equal his Message; Walk must be commensurate with Talk.
20. "Always go for the High Road in dealing with people or issues, do not stay on the Low road." (Apostle Philip Mohabir)

CHAPTER NINE
THE NON-NEGOTIABLES

The late Apostle Mohabir lived beyond his times because of the consuming Vision of the Master that was given to him. I believe, with all my heart that he was willing to work to his last breath to make it happen. That, he did.

1. Team.
   He did not only teach but lived this. In what I deem a manual for all ministers, his book, "Hands of Jesus," he very strongly wrote on it. He concluded the book with team.

   Together
   Each
   Accomplish
   More

   He also emphasized the Golden Principles of every Team.

   - Covenant
   - Care
   - Communication
   - Commitment

- Complement not competition

I also like the way Stephen A. Macchia puts it in his book, "Becoming a Healthy Team"

He called it the Traits of a Healthy Team found in First Corinthians 12:

T rust
E mpowered
A ssimilated
M anaged
S erve

2. The *Five* pillars for Building. (the late Apostle Mohabir)

  * Vision
  * Mission
  * Strategy
  * Values
  * Structure

3. Pray! Pray! Pray!
4. Pioneering
5. Serving others
6. Social action to make the community feel the impact of love and Care.
   Ministry that is aware of the "felt needs". Being relevant.
7. Plurality of leadership.
8. Body ministry

9. Being relevant......like the sons of Issachar, who understood the times and knew what to do.
10. Smart goals: these are the qualitative and quantitative objectives that we feel God wants us to accomplish.

As I look over the past fifty years, these are some of the essentials that I have gathered that have been contributary to us accomplishing all that was done with so meagre resources at first. Our leaders must be honored and commended.

11. To Fulfill Your GIFTINGS, ONE MUST be in…..SHAPE. (Pastor Rick Warren, "Purpose Driven Life"

S piritual Gifts
H eart
A bilities
P ersonality
E xperience

The *SMART Acronym* identifies the qualities the Goals must possess:

S pecific
M easurable
A ttainable
R esults-orientd
T ime-dated. Need for Deadlines.

NOTE: There has been a lot of emphasis on RELATIONSHIP and FELLOWSHIP, and rightly so,

BUT I would beg to suggest that we add FRIENDSHIP to the List. My own story was permeated with some Friendships that helped me in the early days, and even now. We will remember that Jesus Himself called His Disciples Friends.

Some time ago there was a survey done of 18 large churches. The question was asked if the Pastor you loved so much leaves will you stay, and why. It is said that 78% of the people said we will stay because We Have Friends Here.

THE CONCLUSION.......
MY PRAYER

I PRAY, first of all like I see in the conclusion of the Acts of the Apostles, that there will be no end to the story, that this Vision and Mission will continue to grow and expand even greater than it has ever been from generation to generation, as long as the Lord tarries.

I PRAY that the successors will not seek to make changes for change sake to prove a point. That, they would keep the Vision and perpetuate it. It has brought us to this point after 50 years. I agree some of the Methods and Strategies and even Structures may change but the Values are unchangeable. Value of Teams, Relationships, Commitment, Prayer, Purity, Faith. Evangelism etc. are not replaceable. I am aware that you want to eventually instill your Ethos, no problem, that will surely happen as you serve the people for the Glory of the King of kings.

I PRAY that they will only want to move *FORWARD*. I always think that if Rastafarians got one thing right they got the philosophy, *"Forward ever, Backward never!"*

The Acronym for *FORWARD* may help us to stay focused.

F aith, without which no man can please God. This will determine the Future.

O rdinary, God usually raises up Ordinary people to do Extraordinary things.

R esiliency, nothing can beat Deter-mi-nation.

W orship, our first and greatest Ministry; Whole-hearted Prayer.

A ttitude, some one rightly said, Attitude makes for Altitude.

R emember, like David, remembering what God had done inspired him to take on the Giant.

D ecision, determines Destiny. You Receive what you Perceive.

Finally, I pray, that we will ever be Grateful to God for allowing us at different junctures to be and play a part of His program for Redemption of Sinful man. We will always remember and be thankful for all those who labored at the Beginning to lay such a formidable foundation that has been holding up the building for all these Decades. For all who are now faithfully running with the VISION, and those who will take the baton after us.

THE LORD DESIRES GRATITUDE! Let us remember that when the one leper returned to give thanks, Jesus asked,

"Where are the Nine?"

TO HIM BE ALL THE GLORY AND HONOR AND POWER FOREVER AND EVER, AMEN!

Apostle Lionel and Pastor Margaret Etwaru

Printed in Great Britain
by Amazon.co.uk, Ltd.,
Marston Gate.